Snack Boards

Quick and Easy Snack Board Recipes

Copyright © 2020

All rights reserved.

DEDICATION

Contents

Light Cheese Board

prep time 15 minutes

cook time 10 minutes

total time 25 minutes

servings 8

calories 373 kcal

INGREDIENTS

8 ounces fresh burrata cheese

olive oil, for drizzling

1 cup cherry tomatoes, halved

kosher salt and pepper

1 block feta cheese

honey, for drizzling

marinated goat cheese (recipe follows)

6 ounces prosciutto, torn

fruits, veggies, olives, and whole grain crackers, for serving

MARINATED GOAT CHEESE

1/3 cup olive oil

2 sprigs fresh thyme

2 sprigs fresh oregano

1 clove garlic, smashed

1/2 teaspoon crushed red pepper flakes

the rind of 1 lemon

8 ounces goat cheese

INSTRUCTIONS

1. Place the burrata in a small bowl. Drizzle with olive oil and top with tomatoes. Season lightly with salt and pepper.

2. Place the feta cheese on a cheese board or serving platter. Drizzle with honey and top with fresh cherries. Arrange the burrata and marinated goat cheese around the feta. Arrange the prosciutto, fruits, veggies, and crackers around the cheese. EAT!

MARINATED GOAT CHEESE

1. In a small sauce pan, heat the olive oil, thyme, oregano, garlic, and red pepper flakes over medium low heat until fragrant, about 10 minutes. Remove from the heat and stir in the lemon zest and a pinch of salt. Let cool.

2. Roll the goat cheese into small balls and place in a serving bowl or glass jar. Gently pour the oil over the goat cheese. Serve or place in the fridge and chill for up to 2 days.

Beautiful Appetizer Platter

Mmmm, chocolate, candied nuts, fresh cheeses and fruit? Sounds like the perfect combination of my friends' favorite things.

Ingredients

1. **Dried fruit** – I chose dried apricots for this platter. I cut the larger pieces in half so it's nicer as one bite. Other good options would be dried peaches or pears (consider slicing in half or smaller), dried cherries or dried figs.

2. **Fresh fruit** – I used black grapes and mandarin oranges. Other good options include any grapes (even a couple different varieties on the same platter), strawberries, kiwi, blackberries or large raspberries. Apples or pears are a nice choice if you are able to wait to slice them until just before serving (so they don't turn brown before being enjoyed).

3. **Cheese** – I included Gouda, sharp white cheddar and cranberry goat cheese on the platter shown. Choose good quality cheeses that will taste good at room temperature. Lower quality cheeses can sometimes get a little dry and/or greasy when left at room temperature very long. There is a nearly unlimited list of cheeses that would work well on this type of platter. My family likes more mild cheeses, so that's what I usually do. The goat cheese is mostly for me, because I love it! =) I generally slice the cheeses into little "sticks" so they're easy to grab, and easy to eat.

4. **Chocolate** – This is the beautiful little surprise on an otherwise

quite healthy tray. On the tray shown I used Ghirardelli Dark Chocolate with Toffee and Milk Chocolate with Almonds (sold in large bars in the candy isle at the grocery store) and I also included Chocolate Covered Almonds (with sea salt) from Trader Joes. Again, this is a category with unlimited options. I often like to include chocolate covered fruit, such as chocolate covered cherries. I love the variety of choices at Trader Joes, but most any nice grocery store (or even Target) will have some good choices.

5. **Nuts** – I added Dry Roasted (reduced salt) Almonds from Trader Joe's. Any lightly salted nut, or variety of mixed nuts would work perfectly nicely.

6. **Garnish** – I added sprigs of fresh rosemary, simply because I have it in my yard. This is optional, but I do love the added color and texture on the platter. Another nice option would be grape leaves (preferably leaves you know have not been sprayed with pesticides), or any organic, edible flowers (likely more available in the spring and summer). Also, a pretty garnish option would be to include some candies on the platter that are wrapped in a shiny foil wrapper (such as Hershey's Kisses, etc). The bright foil would be a pretty element.

INSTRUCTIONS

1. Wash, slice, peel (as appropriate) the fruit and lay out of a clean

towel to dry. As appropriate, use the towel to dry the fruit. You don't want excess water from the fruit getting onto other elements on the platter.

2. Slice the cheeses, as desired.

3. Begin assembly by adding the fruit, then cheeses in sections on the platter. Group items together, but you can have more than one section of the same items (you'll see two sections of grapes, and two sections of mandarin segments on the platter pictured).

4. Continue filling in the platter by adding sections of dried fruit, then the nuts and chocolates. Keep color in mind as you assemble. You'll see that on the platter pictured, I've spread the orange colored elements, as well as the purple, brown, and lighter colored elements somewhat evenly around the platter.

5. Add garnish, as appropriate. I added the rosemary last, but if you are using grape leaves or something on the bottom of the platter, obviously you'll need to add that earlier.

A few things to consider...

Cost – This type of appetizer tray can get quite expensive to make. The fruit will likely be the least expensive item (relative to the amount of space it takes up on the platter), so if you want to keep the cost down, add more fruit and reserve less space for other items.

Crackers – Certainly crackers would be a nice accompaniment to this platter. I usually prefer to serve a smaller plate of assorted crackers separate from this fruit & cheese platter mainly because I do not want the moisture from the fruit and cheese to affect the crackers.

Prep Time – The bulk of the prep required for this time of tray can be done ahead of time (such as a day in advance). You can slice the cheeses and dried fruit and store appropriately. Also, some of the fruit (especially grapes) could be washed and cut into small bunches ahead of time. Once you have the elements for your platter selected, and cut (as needed), the assembly itself should not take long a all.

Holiday Cheese Board

Thanksgiving and Christmas are not so far away and with it comes a lot of entertaining! Show your festive side with a holiday themed cheese board.

Step 1: Selecting your cheeses

I always like to have a wide variety of cheeses because everyone is different in what they prefer, but I like to serve about 3 to 5 different types on my board. A few staples to have are a soft cheese like brie or semi-soft such as havarti, a firmer cheese such as aged cheddar, fontina or smoked gouda, and I also like to throw on a strong blue cheese as well because some people just love it! For this particular cheeseboard I partnered with Castello Cheese and used a variety of their Creamy Havarti, Extra Mature Cheddar, Extra Creamy Danish Blue, and Havarti Jalapeno for some added spice!

I like to cut my cheeses in different ways too, which makes styling the board much more fun! Cut your firmer cheeses into cubes, the softer cheeses into slices and I like to leave the brie and blue cheeses whole, crumbling the blue just a bit to give the overall board some texture. You really can't go wrong though because no matter what you do, it's a beautiful mess!

Step 2: Perfect pairings

That's right, every cheeseboard needs delicious accompaniments and

I always like to have the perfect mix of sweet and savory. Here are some ideas for those little extra pairings:

Sweet – This can include fresh fruit like grapes, apples, pears, etc., (but make sure to keep it seasonal!), dried fruit like cranberries or raisins, and a dollop of honey also tastes perfect on top of brie or other soft cheeses. I also like to use different types of spreads and for this board I used my favorite fig and orange jam along with homemade sweet and spicy cranberry salsa which tasted incredible on top of cheese and crackers! You can find the recipe for this salsa below.

Savory – Here's where you add your favorite charcuterie! I love to use a mix of spicy salami and prosciutto along with some Marcona almonds and candied walnuts. Olives are great to add to your cheeseboard as well, but I ended up making the cranberry salsa, rather than a tapenade, for some fun holiday flare.

Step 3: Your cheese needs a vehicle

I mean hey you could totally go to town and just grab your cheese as-is (hey I'm liking your style!), but every cheeseboard needs a variety of crackers to place that cheesy goodness on! For this board I used some basic round crackers, some crunchy bread sticks and Lesley Stowe's Raincoast Crisps that I am legit utterly OBSESSED with!!

Seriously guys these are THE best crackers and have so many different flavors to choose from giving you that perfect salty/sweet bite. My current favorites are the pumpkin spice and the cranberry hazelnut crackers, but for this board I went with rosemary raisin pecan crackers because UM amazing.

Step 4: Garnish, garnish, garnish!

This part is so important for displaying your killer holiday cheeseboard and it also fills in any of those little holes or gaps you have leftover to complete the overall look! Make sure to choose garnishes that go with the season, so for example I added sprigs of rosemary and juicy pomegranate seeds which added a pretty pop of color, but I also placed a little greenery and pine cones around the sides just to give the display a little something extra. Your guests will be impressed and it sure makes everything that much more appetizing!

Step 5: Pour the wine

Every great cheese display needs a bottle or two of wine to go with it! Some of my favorite wine pairings are Cabernet Sauvignon, Pinot Noir, Sauvignon Blanc, and a bubbly prosecco, but since we're diving into the winter months, I served Folie à Deux Pinot Noir which paired perfectly with all the flavors on this board.

Learn how to create the perfect holiday cheese board in just five simple steps with an assortment of cheeses, meats, fruits, nuts, and a variety of spreads!

Now that your cheeseboard is assembled, it's time to dig in!

Here's a quick little tip: I always like to set my cheeseboard out at room temperature for about 30 minutes to an hour before serving because this makes the cheese much softer and SO much more flavorful. Plus I mean who wants to eat cold cheese??

Okay so let's talk about this sweet and spicy cranberry salsa!! I just love this recipe because it is super fun for the holidays and tastes delicious with crackers, bread and, yes you guessed it, CHEESE! You could either make this recipe as-is and simply use it as a topping OR you could easily mix the salsa with a block of cream cheese and make more of a spread. The possibilities are endless, but I promise it will look gorgeous on your cheeseboard and be a huge hit either way you serve it!

Just a warning though.....it's super addictive.

Turkey Snack Board

How to make a festive and delicious Turkey Snack Board for everyone to gobble up at your Thanksgiving gatherings!

Prep Time: 30 mins

Total Time: 30 mins

INGREDIENTS

1 brown Bosc pear

variety of scalloped crackers

cheddar cheese cracker cuts

green grapes

red grapes

red apple slices

green apple slices

roasted almond

candied walnuts

dried apricots

baby carrots

snow peas

dried cherries

macadamia nut halves, for eyes

red bell pepper, for snood

honey, for sticking items to pear

INSTRUCTIONS

1. Use a 15-inch round wooden board or any round board or serving platter you have.

2. Cut the brown Bosc pear in half and place the cut side down at the bottom of the board.

3. From the pear, fan out all of the snacks to look like turkey feathers. The scalloped crackers first and then two lines of the cheese cracker cuts between the lines of crackers.

4. On the left half of the board, add the green grapes, red apple slices, roasted almonds, baby carrots, snow peas, and dried cherries to fill the left side in.

5. On the right side of the board, add the red grapes, green apple slices, candied walnuts, dried apricots, snow peas and dried cherries to fill the right side in.

6. For the eyes, use two macadamia nut halves with a piece of dried cherry stuck to the middle of the flat side of each one. Place them on the pear, flat side up, with a little honey to hold them in place.

7. For the beak, cut a corner off of one of the cheddar cracker cuts and place it on the pear upside down.

8. For the snood, cut a small piece of a red bell pepper or red apple and place it on the pear under the beak with a little honey.

9. And for the feet, place two candied pecans at the bottom of the pear with a little honey so they stick in place.

10.   Serve and enjoy!

Football Party Snack Board

Across the US, millions of people love to watch football, and all that the game has to offer. If you are often in charge of cooking for these ever-important live events, then we've got a game-changer for you.

This awe-inspiring snack board offers all the best flavors of finger foods like carrots celery, cheese, chips, and of course, crispy chicken wings. Use your creativity and add in what your family and friends love.

CHICKEN WINGS

Chicken wings are the quintessential game day party appetizer. They're easy to pick up and eat, and they come in a multitude of flavors. Classic buffalo wings are a must, but these brown butter honey wings add another delicious flavor profile. With these two recipes you get a dry, breaded option as well as a saucy option.

Other options that would be just as welcome are these teriyaki chicken fingers w/ peanut dipping sauce and these football party food pigskin poppers.

I've added the two different flavors to my football themed snack board, and placed them at opposite corners to help frame the wood board. It's a good trick of the trade that keeps the eye moving.

CRUDITES

No party is complete without a variety of fresh vegetables, or crudites. They give a healthy alternative to the spread, as well as act as a palate cleanser between bites. Choices here include carrot sticks, celery sticks, and green beans. The beans are slightly steamed so they're not raw but still have a firm texture and crunch.

Add two dips that will accommodate the chicken wings and the vegetables for dipping. Obvious choices are blue cheese dressing and ranch dressing.

HOSTESS TIP: Add some crumbled blue cheese to the blue cheese dressing to pump up the flavor and texture.

CHIPS

I'm a chip junkie so every football party has to have some crispy crunchy chips! Here I've included two flavor varieties. These are terrific to add to your snack board and you can dunk them in the dips too.

Easy Fall Apple and Cheese Board

How to make a simple Fall Apple and Cheese Board that is perfect as a snack or party platter! This cheese board recipe is so great because it can be served as a light dinner, or as an easy appetizer.

INGREDIENTS

Smoked Gouda, Jarlsberg (similar to Swiss), and Peppercorn Cheddar

honey

The Best Caramel Dip (1 cup)

whole grain mustard

red and green apples, whole and sliced

caramel candies

dried apples

assorted crackers

mini pretzels

apple and/or fall leaves for garnish

board

cheese knives

INSTRUCTIONS

1. Place your cheeses on your board. Feel free to pre-slice one of the cheeses if you desire.
2. Place condiments (caramel sauce, honey, and mustard) in small serving bowls and place on board.
3. Place crackers and pretzels around the cheeses.
4. Add a few whole apples and lots of apple slices.
5. Fill in the gaps with dried apples and caramel candies.
6. Garnish with leaves.
7. Serve right away.

Winter Cheese Board

Now that we've settled when seasons change, we shall declare that creating this vibrant and handsome winter cheese board is a must this

December. The fresh clementine, dried figs, and pickles help create a colorful array of fresh food components.

The toasted walnuts and pungent cheeses are perfectly paired with sweet honeycomb. Oh my, are you hungry yet? As if this board isn't pretty enough, you can further embellish it with fresh sprigs of rosemary. Pop open a bottle of your finest red and enjoy this fancy spread.

Prep Time: 15 mins

Total Time: 15 mins

INGREDIENTS

1 square of honeycomb

4 ounces sliced merlot Bellavitano (Sartori)

4 ounces sliced rosemary Asiago

4 ounces Gorgonzola

2 ounces sliced aged Parmesan

2 clementines, peeled and segmented

½ cup Castelvetrano olives

½ cup toasted walnuts

½ cup cornichons

4 dried figs, halved

Rosemary sprigs, for garnish (optional)

Crackers or homemade pita chips

Red wine of choice

INSTRUCTIONS

1. Arrange honeycomb and cheeses around corners of board, slightly fanning cheese slices.
2. Fill in large areas with clementines, olives, and walnuts then fill in smaller areas with cornichons, figs and rosemary sprigs (if using).
3. Serve with crackers or pita chips and red wine, of course.

NOTES

- Don't like blue cheese? No problem, swap in a soft cheese like goat cheese or even Brie. Not a fan of dried figs? Add dried apricots, or cherries. Use this recipe as a guide for amounts and flavor pairings, then make it your own with your favorite ingredients.

Grilled Fruit Cheese Board

Sinking your teeth into a juicy hunk of char-grilled fruit is nothing short of delicious. Grilling fruit like apples, pears, and pineapple is super easy, and the recipes available out there are endless.

Take a flour tortilla wedge, place a grilled fruit slice on top accompanied with a slice of cheese and drizzle it with honey. Once you take a bite of exquisite combination, you'll never look back.

prep time: 15 MINUTES

cook time: 10 MINUTES

total time: 25 MINUTES

INGREDIENTS

3 tablespoons olive oil

Peach, sliced

Avocado, sliced

Pear, sliced

Pineapple, sliced

Membrillo, quince paste

Water crackers or crackers or your choice

Flour tortillas, cut into wedges

Honey

Jam or preserves of your choice

Assorted soft and hard cheeses

Fresh herbs: mint and basil

INSTRUCTIONS

1. Slice fruit and brush with olive oil.
2. Place fruit on a grill pan over medium-high heatand grill until fruit is tender, but not mushy. Set aside and cool.
3. Place grilled fruit slices, cheeses, and crackers around the board.
4. Add in herbs and flowers for color.

NOTES

- I recommend brushing slices of fruit with some olive oil and grilling the fruit on a grill pan rather than grilling small slices of fruit on an outdoor grill.

Fruit and Chocolate Dessert Board

Chocolate:

Dark Chocolate Cherry Almond Bark

Dark Chocolate Pineapple Almond Ginger Bark

28

White Chocolate Cranberry Pistachio Bark

Orange-Peach Dark Chocolate Bites

Dark Chocolate Almond Blueberry Swiss Bar

Cheese:

French Brie

Cranberry Goat Cheese "heart"

Wine Rubbed Italian Blue Cheese with wine-soaked Cranberries

Vermont Artisan Cheese

Fruit:

Pomegranate

Grapes

Blackberries

Strawberries

Pears

Accompaniments:

Chocolate Cookie Crisps

Chocolate Chip Cookie Crisps

Biscotti

Cinnamon Raisin Bread

Simple water crackers

Hear-shaped donuts (for Valentine's day)

Sugared Pecans

Almonds

Bruschetta Bar

Bruschetta is a beloved appetizer, and it is even more tasty when you can create your own with tons of toppings!

INGREDIENTS

Various cheese (get a mix of flavors, textures, shapes, and colors)

Salty items (meats, nuts, olives, etc.)

Sweet items (fruit, dried fruit, chocolate, etc.)

Crunchy items (crackers, pita chips, breadsticks, etc.)

Condiments (honey, mustards, chutney, etc.)

Space-filling items (grapes, cherry tomatoes, cherries)

Garnish (fresh herbs)

Cheese board (can use a cheese board, cutting board, serving platter, tray, or cookie sheet)

Cheese knives

INSTRUCTIONS

1. Begin by spreading the cheese wedges, logs, and wheels evenly throughout the cheese board surface. Add cheese knives.
2. Next, fill around the cheese with the salty items.
3. Then, add a few piles of sweet items.
4. Pile in the crunchy items and the condiments in small jars or bowls.
5. Next, fill in any empty spaces with space-filling items like grapes, cherry tomatoes, or cherries.
6. Finally, garnish the cheese board with fresh herbs.

Dessert Cheese Plate

Serve up dessert in a way that will allow people to nibble on their favorite sweets all night!

Total Time: 20 minutes

INGREDIENTS

1 Dragon's Breath Blue Cheese Ball, cut in half

nuts

figs, sliced in half

pears, sliced

raspberries

blackberries

little dish of honey

savour jams, like pear and roasted garlic

mini pastries

nougat, cut into bite sized chunks

chocolate

oat crackers (or you favourite crackers)

INSTRUCTIONS

1. Cut the Dragon's Breath Blue cheese in half, and add a little cheese knife for serving.
2. Place the halves in the centre of the cheese plate.
3. Place the remaining ingredients around the cheese. I find to make it most visually appealing, add little piles of the ingredients all around the cheese, as shown in the pictures above.

4. Enjoy!

Cheese and Meat Board

When cheese and meat are the focus, how can you go wrong? Add some dried fruit and nuts into the mix for a flavorfully delicious snack board.

INGREDIENTS

Boursin Cheese

Stilton Cheese

Brie

salumi

prosciutto

olives

sliced pears

dried apricots

raspberries

dried nuts

honey

variety of crackers

INSTRUCTIONS

1. Group, layer and arrange each ingredient in piles.

Antipasto Platter

prep time 30 minutes

cook time 10 minutes

total time 1 hour 40 minutes

INGREDIENTS

15-18 sweet cherry peppers

4 ounces goat cheese

1 pound assorted thinly sliced deli meats (I use prosciutto + soppressata + salami)

1 jar marinated artichokes

1 jar roasted red bell peppers

1 jar oil packed sun-dried tomatoes OR sun-dried tomato pesto

8 ounces fresh mozzarella or buffalo mozzarella rolled in fresh herbs

marinated feta recipe follows

marinated olives recipe follows

1 cup homemade or store bought hummus + olive oil for drizzling

fresh basil + radishes + cherry tomatoes or other fresh veggies

apricots + strawberries + fig jam + honey or other fruits

fresh pita + pita chips + bread sticks or other breads/crackers

MARINATED FETA

6 ounces block feta cut into 1/2 inch cubes

1/4 cup fresh herbs (I like thyme basil, oregano)

pinch of crushed red pepper flakes

olive oil enough to cover the cheese

MARINATED OLIVES

1/2 cup olive oil

6 cloves garlic peeled

2 cups mixed olives I used kalamata and green olives

crushed red pepper flakes to taste

INSTRUCTIONS

2. Take the sweet cherry peppers and gently stuff them with the goat cheese.

3. Arrange all the ingredients on a large platter or wood cutting board. Drizzle a little olive oil over the hummus. Serve with assorted breads and crackers so people can mix and match their bites depending in their tastes.

MARINATED FETA

1. Add the cubed feta, herbs and crushed red pepper to an 8 ounce or larger glass jar.

2. Pour enough olive oil over top so that the oil completely covers the feta. Screw the lid on the jar and place in the fridge for at least one hour or up to two weeks. Just crumble the feta onto whatever you wish.

MARINATED OLIVES

1. Add the olive oil and garlic to a small saucepan and set over medium low heat.

2. Bring the oil to a simmer and then reduce the heat to LOW.

3. Simmer, for 10 minutes, stirring occasionally until fragrant. Remove from the heat, stir in olives.

4. Add crushed red pepper to taste. Can be served warm or chilled. Olives can be stored in a glass jar in the fridge for up to 1 week.

Made in the USA
Las Vegas, NV
12 October 2022

57096939R00025